Essential Pop Hits

15 Timeless Selections
Arranged for Elementary Piano with Optional Duet Accompaniments
By Tom Gerou

Contents

Alfred

Produced by
Alfred Music Publishing Co., Inc.
P.O. Box 10003
Van Nuys, CA 91410-0003
alfred.com

ISBN-10: 0-7390-6943-8
ISBN-13: 978-0-7390-6943-1

Cover Credits
[Fred Flintstone]: TM & © 1997 Hanna-Barbera, All Rights Reserved • [Luke Skywalker]: © Lucasfilm Ltd., All Rights Reserved

As Time Goes By

Words and Music by
Herman Hupfeld

Arranged by Tom Gerou

Optional Duet Accompaniment (Play solo part 1 octave higher than written.)

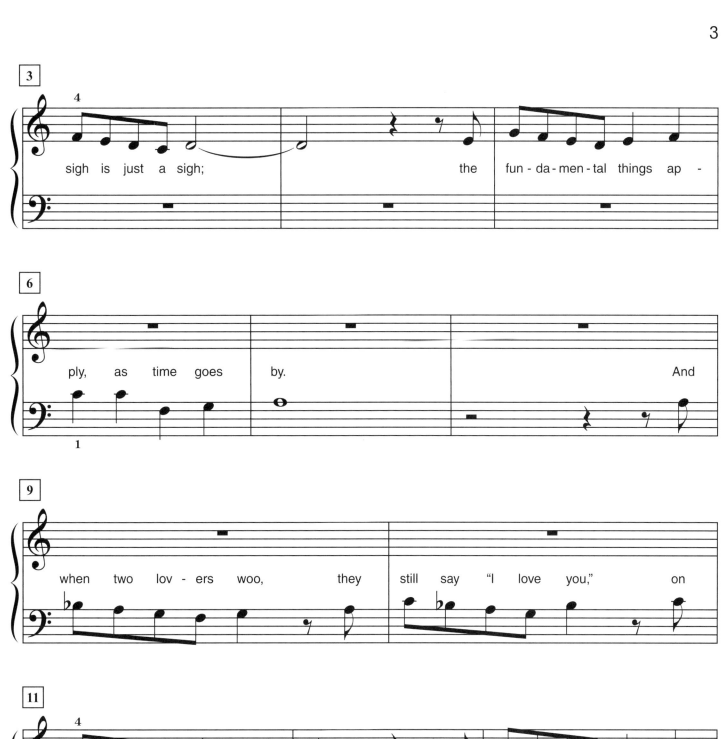

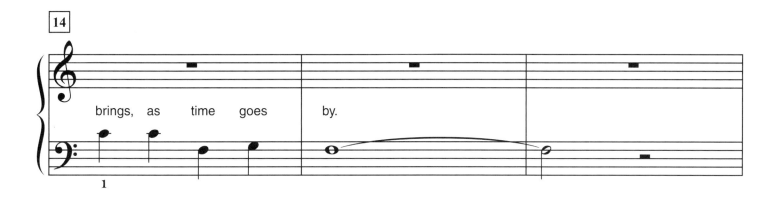

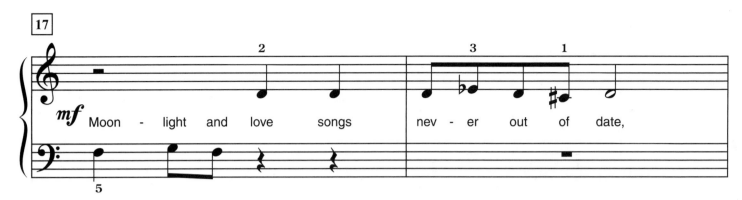

Moon - light and love songs nev - er out of date,

hearts full of pas - sion, jeal - ous - y and hate;

(duet continued)

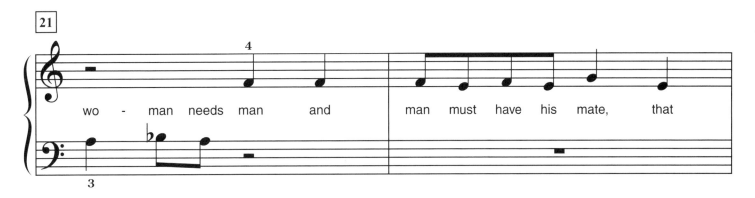

wo - man needs man and man must have his mate, that

no one can de - ny. *mp* It's still the same old sto - ry, a

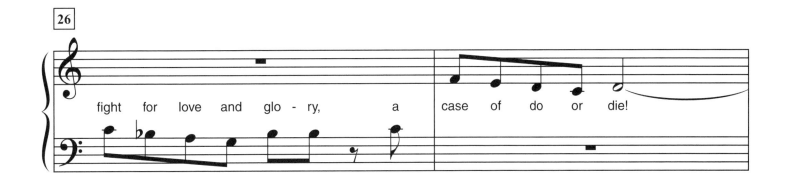

fight for love and glo - ry, a case of do or die!

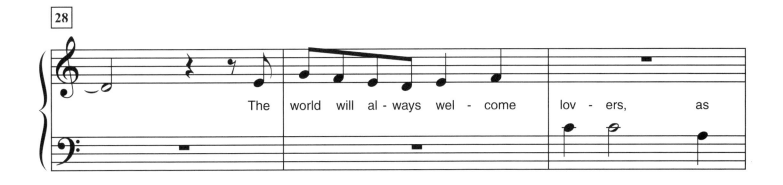

The world will al - ways wel - come lov - ers, as

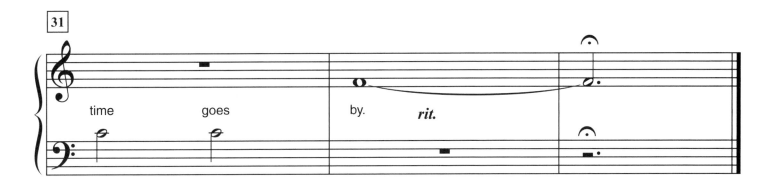

time goes by. *rit.*

(Meet) The Flintstones

Words and Music by
Joseph Barbera, William Hanna and Hoyt Curtin
Arranged by Tom Gerou

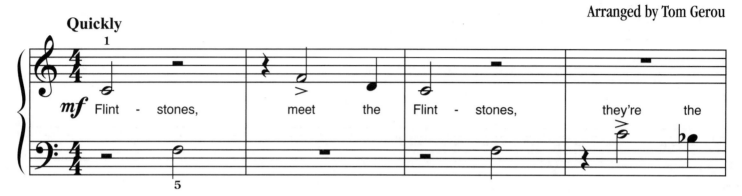

Optional Duet Accompaniment (Play solo part 1 octave higher than written.)

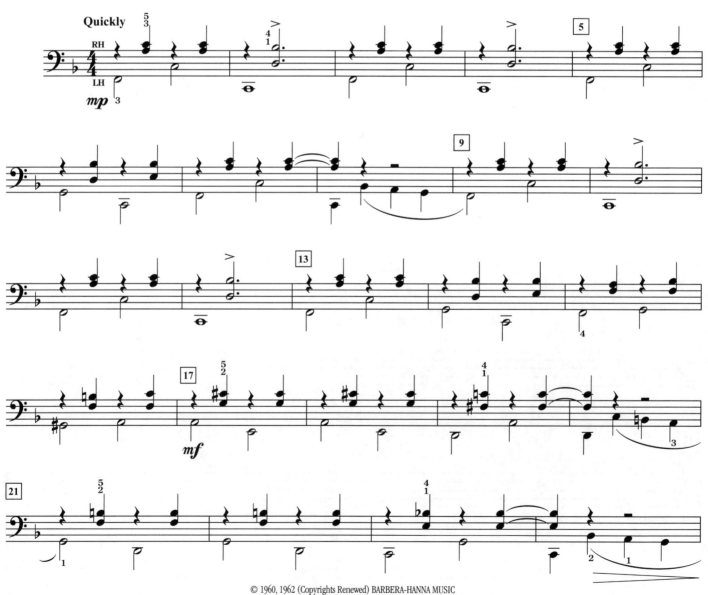

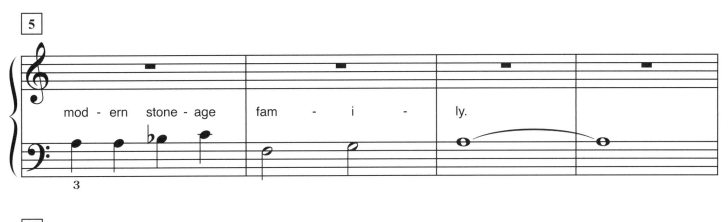

5 mod - ern stone - age fam - i - ly.

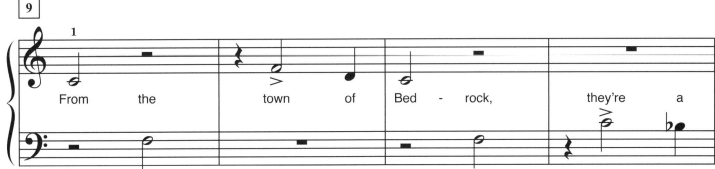

9 From the town of Bed - rock, they're a

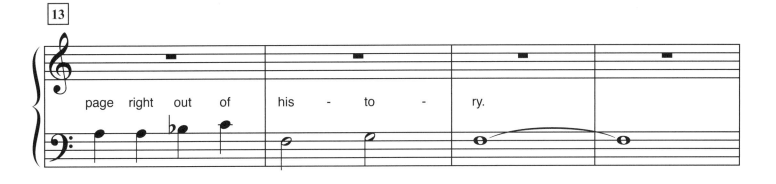

13 page right out of his - to - ry.

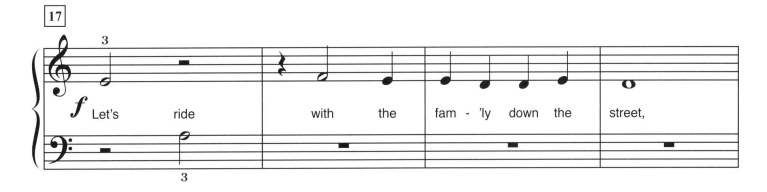

17 *f* Let's ride with the fam - 'ly down the street,

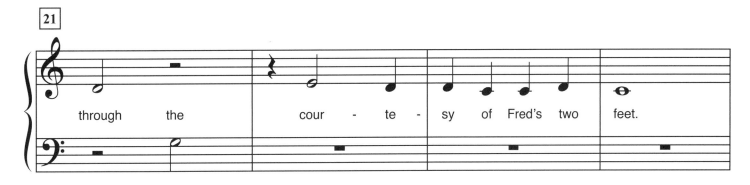

21 through the cour - te - sy of Fred's two feet.

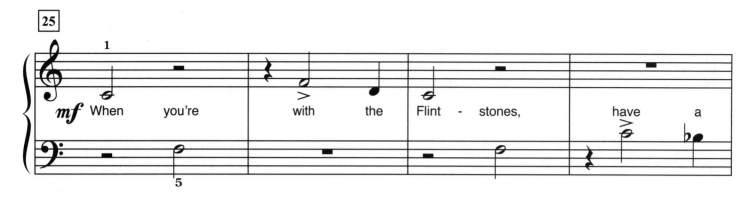

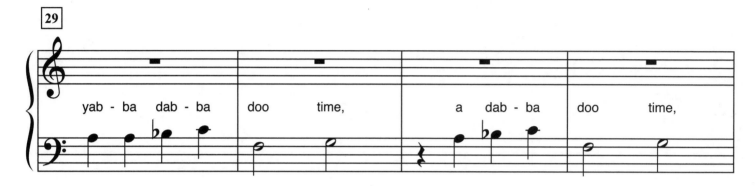

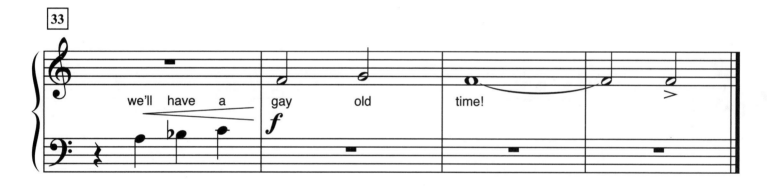

(duet continued)

Gonna Fly Now

By Bill Conti,
Ayn Robbins and Carol Connors
Arranged by Tom Gerou

Optional Duet Accompaniment (Play solo part 1 octave higher than written.)

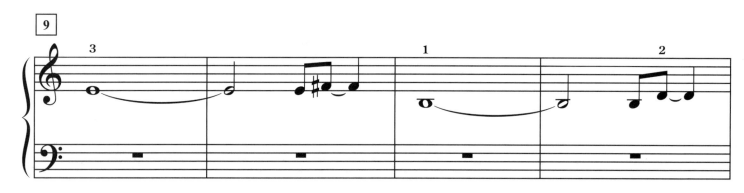

(duet continued)

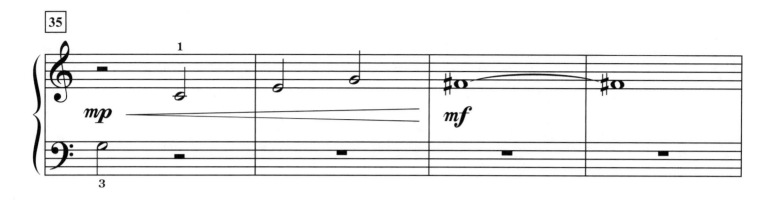

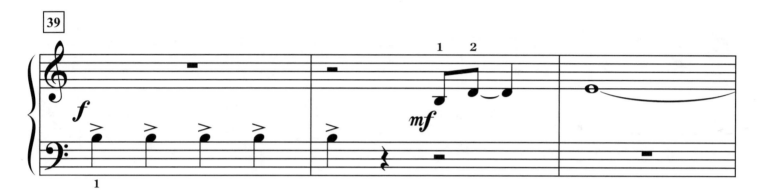

(duet continued)

I Won't Grow Up

Lyrics by Carolyn Leigh
Music by Mark Charlap
Arranged by Tom Gerou

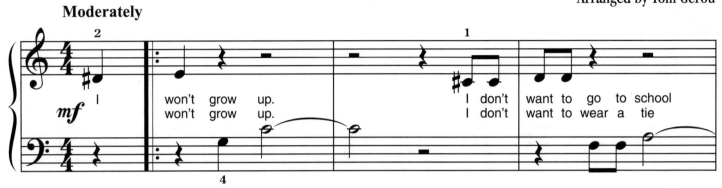

Optional Duet Accompaniment (Play solo part 1 octave higher than written.)

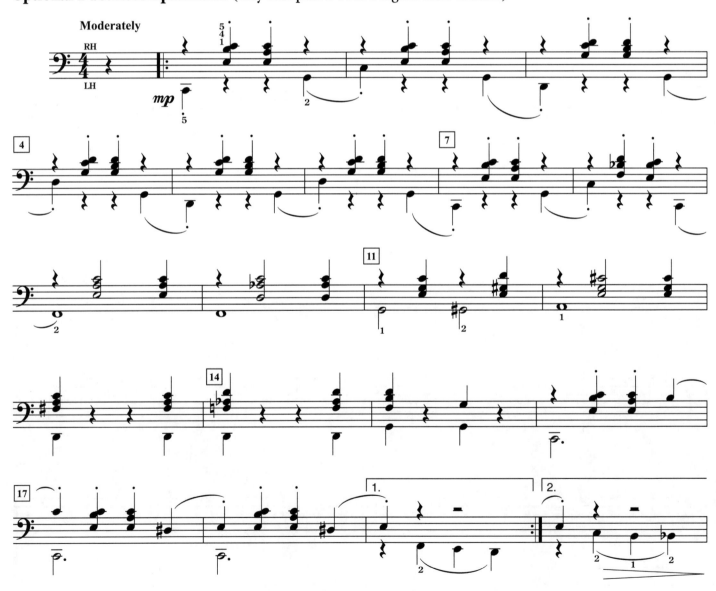

(duet continued)

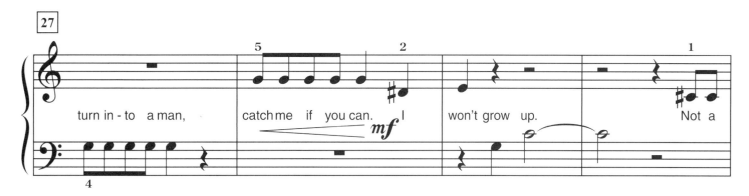

turn in-to a man, catch me if you can. I won't grow up. Not a

pen-ny will I pinch. I will nev-er grow a mus-tache, or a

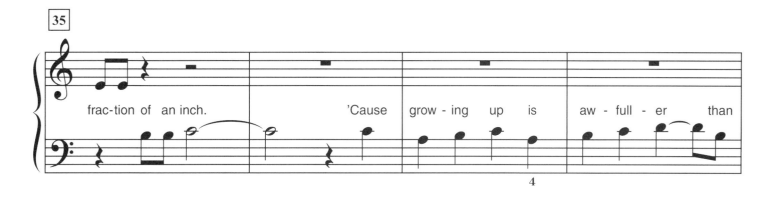

frac-tion of an inch. 'Cause grow-ing up is aw-full-er than

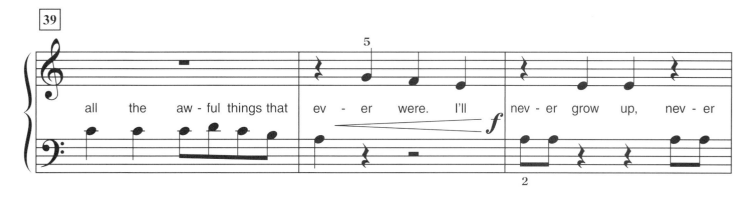

all the aw-ful things that ev - er were. I'll nev - er grow up, nev - er

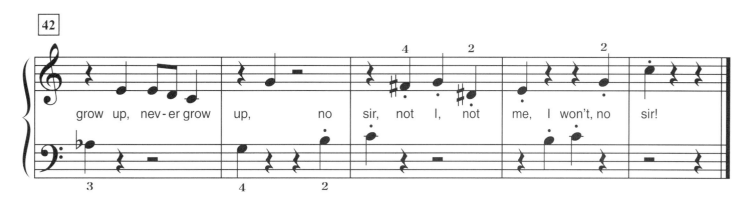

grow up, nev-er grow up, no sir, not I, not me, I won't, no sir!

James Bond Theme

By Monty Norman

Arranged by Tom Gerou

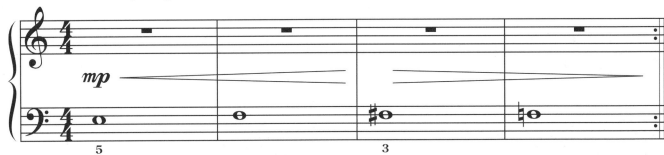

Optional Duet Accompaniment (Play solo part 1 octave higher than written.)

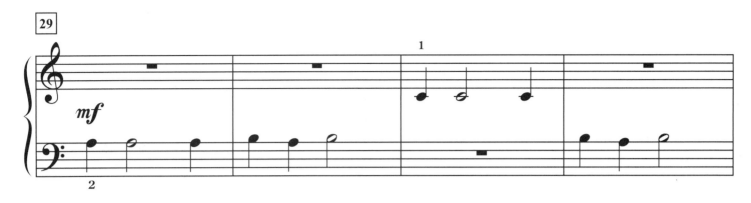

(duet continued)

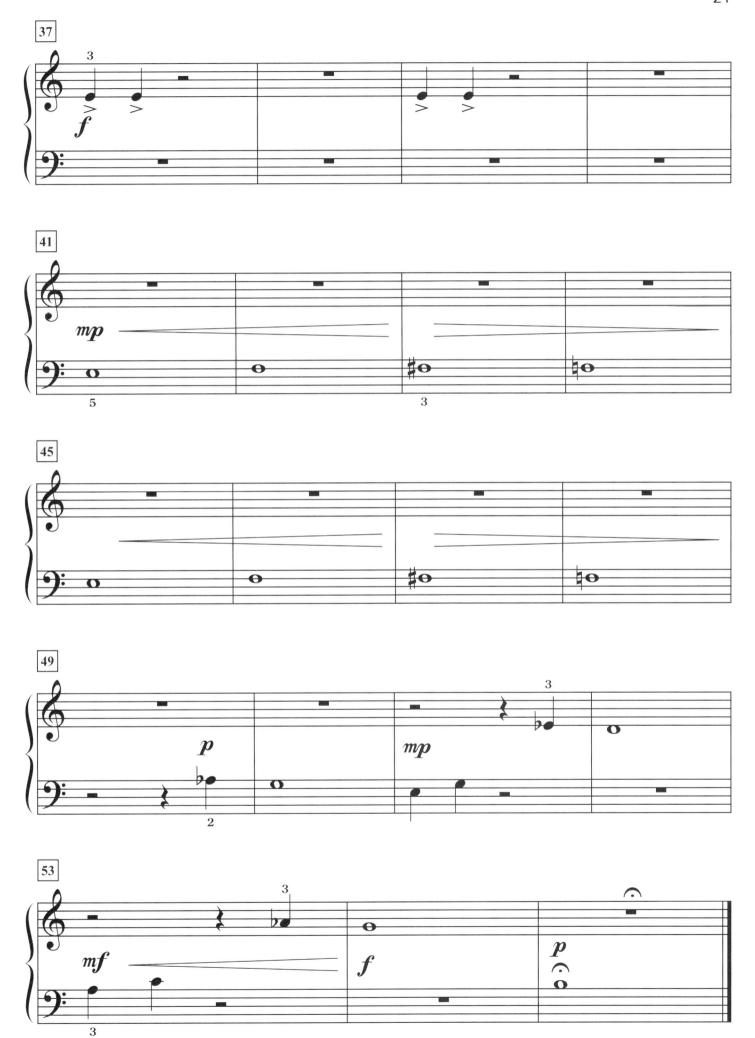

Theme from *New York, New York*

Words by Fred Ebb
Music by John Kander
Arranged by Tom Gerou

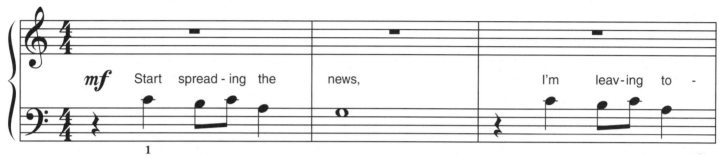

Start spread-ing the news, I'm leav-ing to -

Optional Duet Accompaniment (Play solo part 1 octave higher than written.)

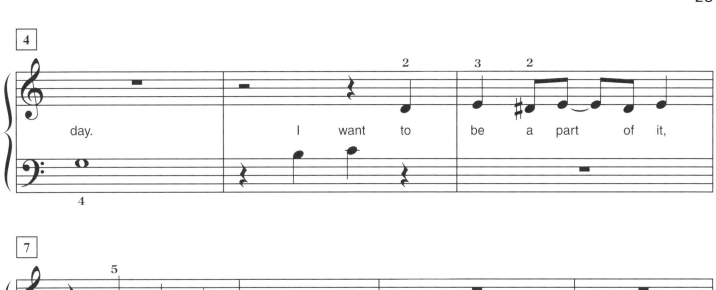
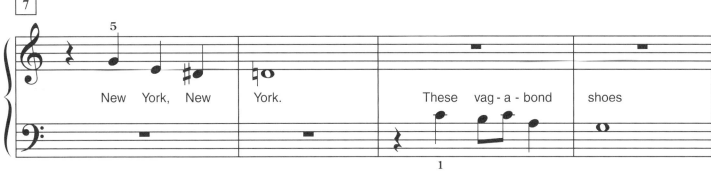
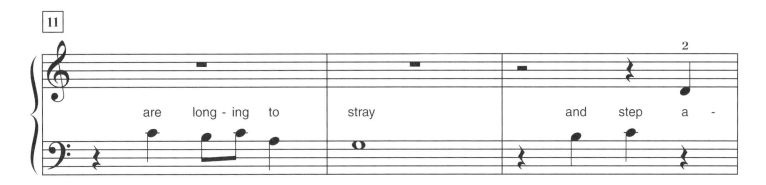
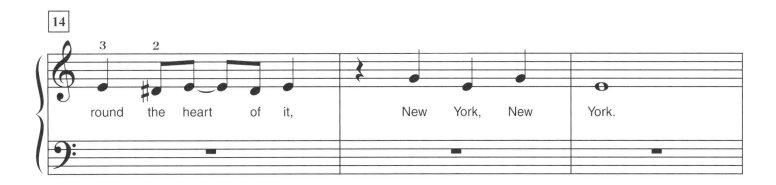

23

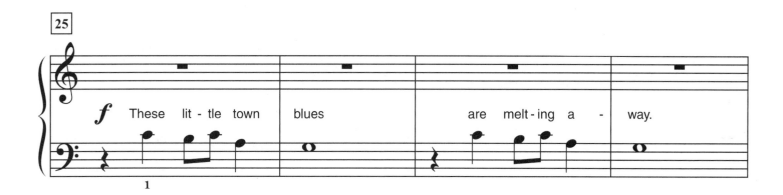

(duet continued)

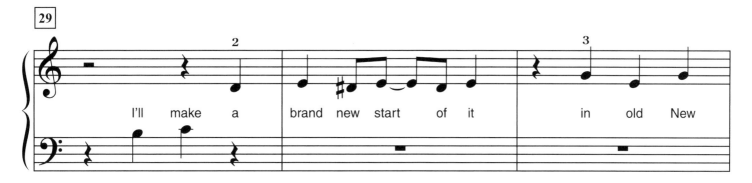

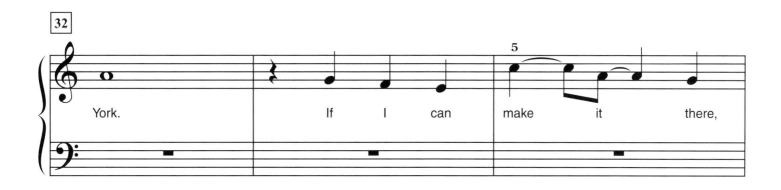

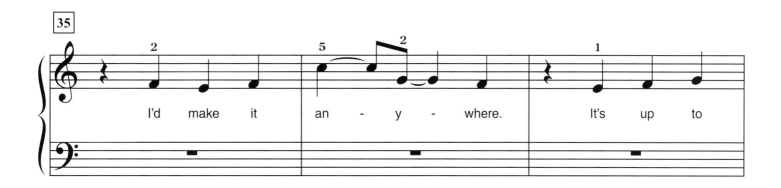

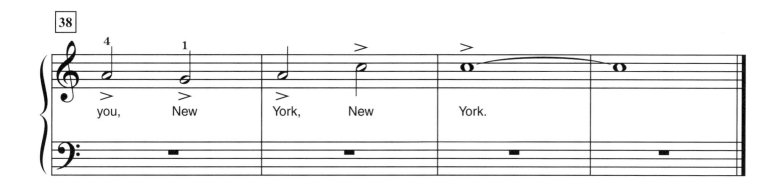

Over the Rainbow

Lyrics by E. Y. Harburg
Music by Harold Arlen
Arranged by Tom Gerou

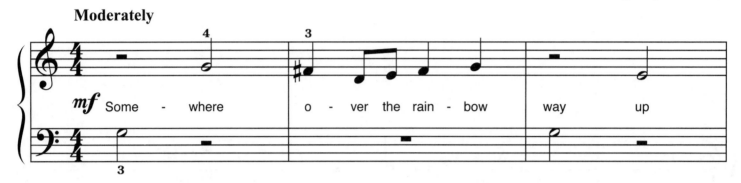

Optional Duet Accompaniment (Play solo part 1 octave higher than written.)

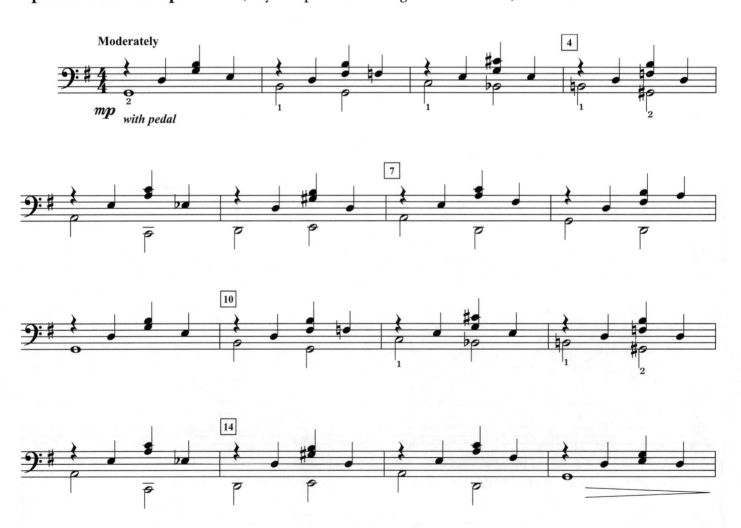

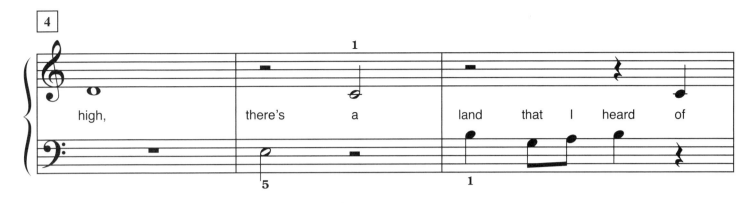

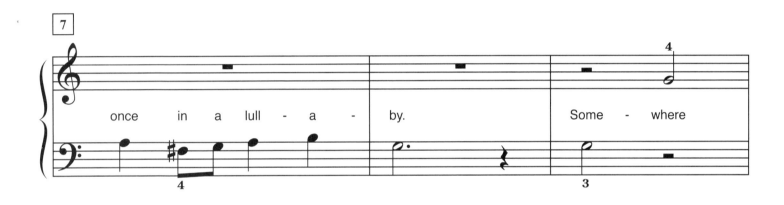

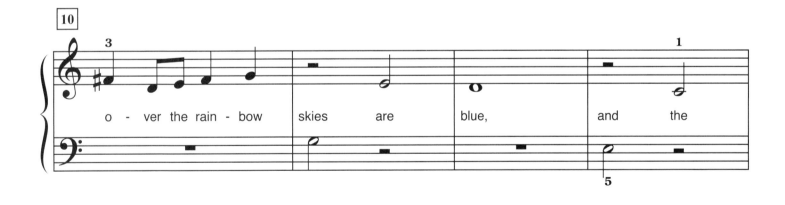

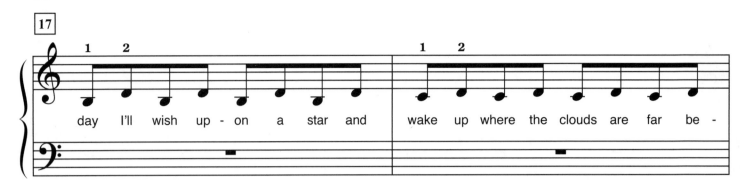

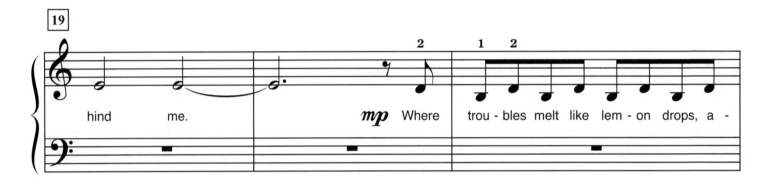

(duet continued)

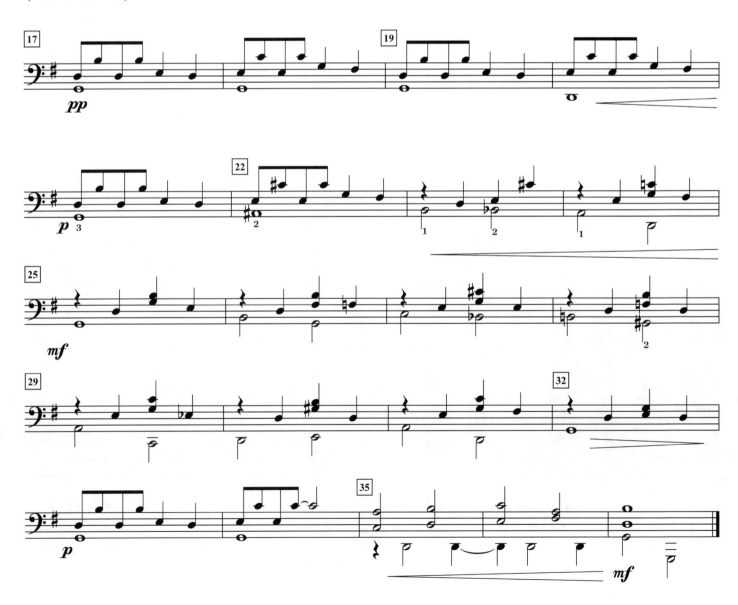

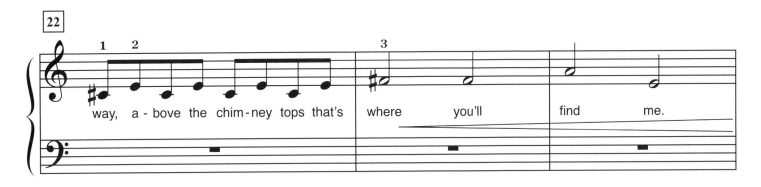

way, a-bove the chim-ney tops that's where you'll find me.

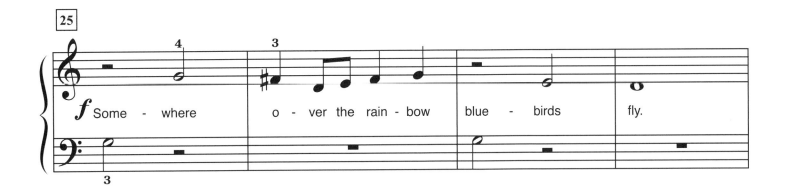

f Some-where o-ver the rain-bow blue-birds fly.

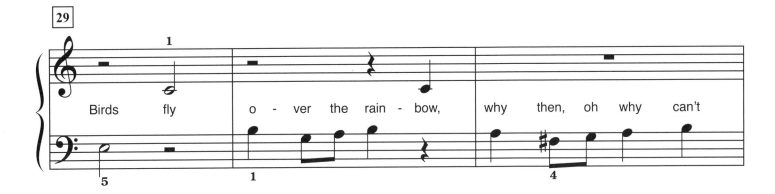

Birds fly o-ver the rain-bow, why then, oh why can't

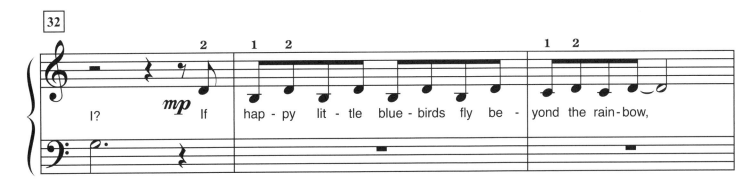

I? *mp* If hap-py lit-tle blue-birds fly be-yond the rain-bow,

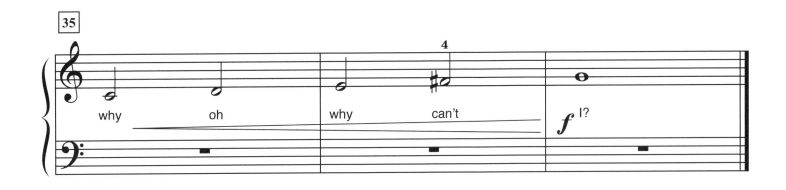

why oh why can't *f* I?

The Pink Panther

By Henry Mancini

Arranged by Tom Gerou

Optional Duet Accompaniment (Play solo part 1 octave higher than written.)

The Rose

Words and Music by
Amanda McBroom

Arranged by Tom Gerou

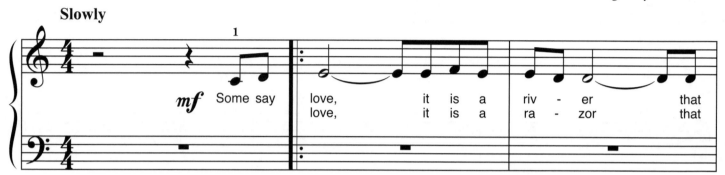

Optional Duet Accompaniment (Play solo part 1 octave higher than written.)

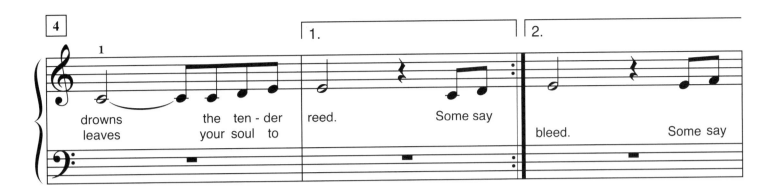

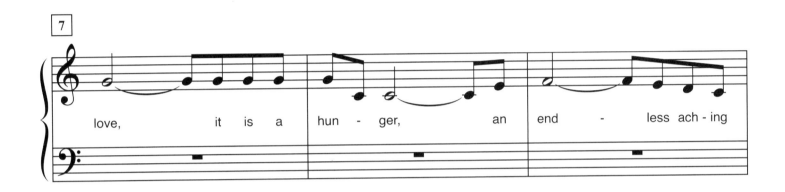

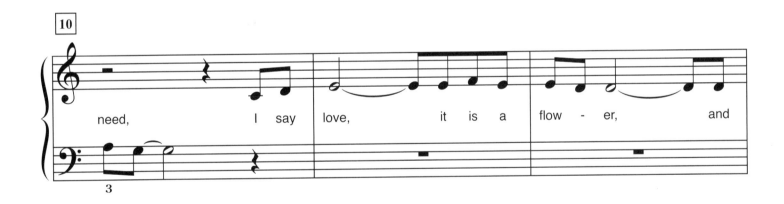

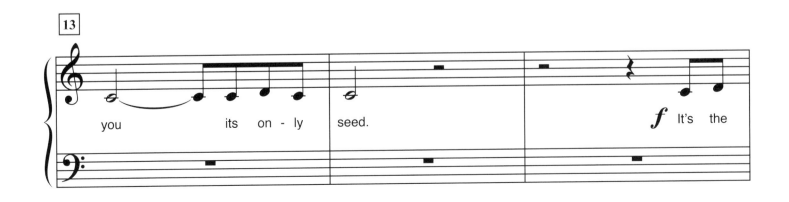

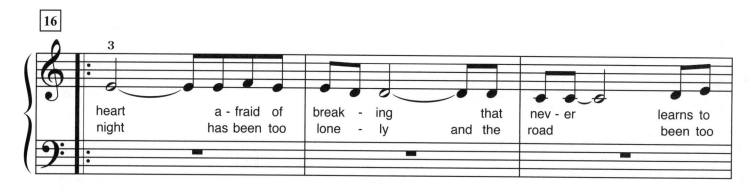

heart   a - fraid of   break - ing   that   nev - er   learns to
night   has been too   lone - ly   and the   road   been too

dance.   It's the   dream   a - fraid of   wak - ing   that
long,   and you   think   that love is   on - ly   for the

(duet continued)

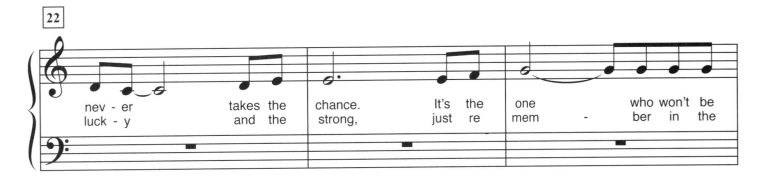

22 nev - er takes the chance. It's the one who won't be
luck - y and the strong, just re mem - ber in the

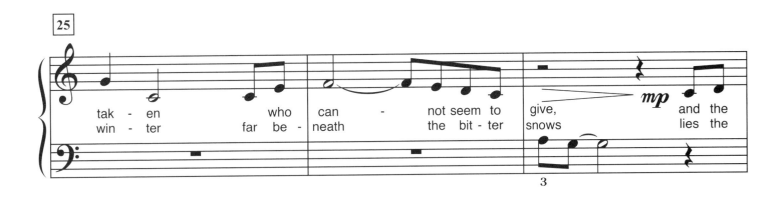

25 tak - en who can - not seem to give, *mp* and the
win - ter far be - neath the bit - ter snows lies the

3

28 soul a - fraid of dy - ing that nev - er learns to live.
seed that with the sun's love in the

1.

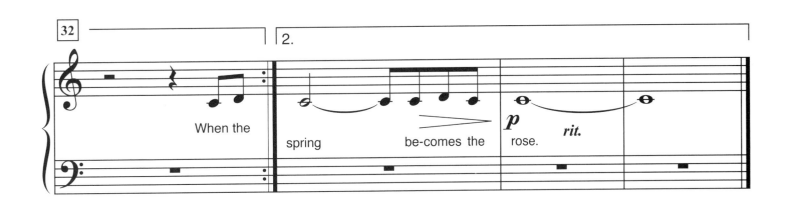

32 When the
spring be-comes the *p* rose. *rit.*

2.

Summertime

Music and Lyrics by
George Gershwin, Ira Gershwin and
DuBose and Dorothy Heyward
Arranged by Tom Gerou

Optional Duet Accompaniment (Play solo part 1 octave higher than written.)

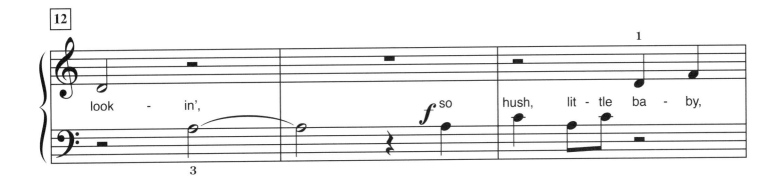

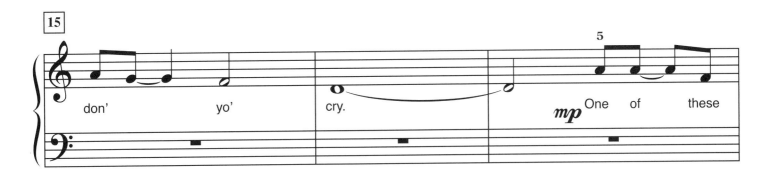

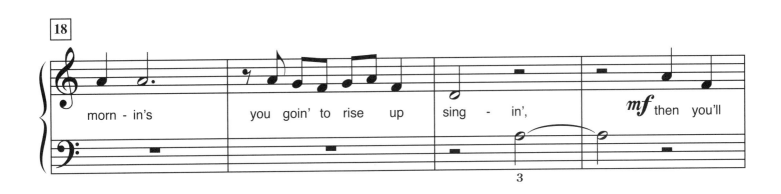

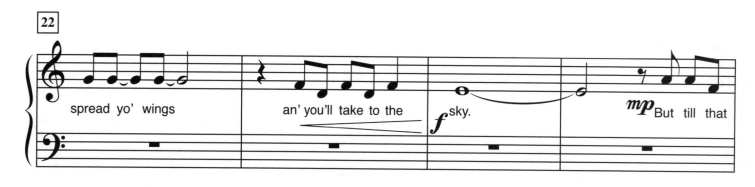

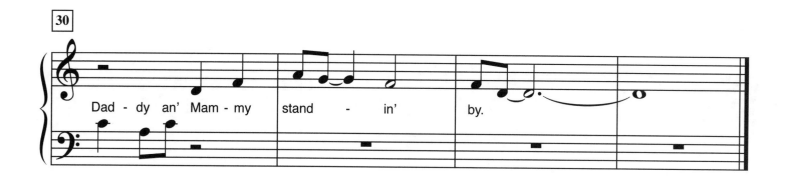

(duet continued)

(We're Gonna) Rock Around the Clock

Words and Music by
Max C. Freedman and Jimmy De Knight
Arranged by Tom Gerou

Optional Duet Accompaniment (Play solo part 1 octave higher than written.)

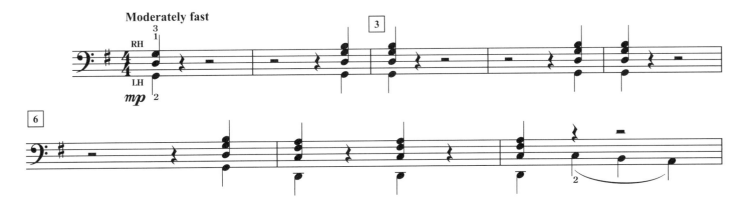

glad rags on and   join me, hon, we'll   have some fun when the

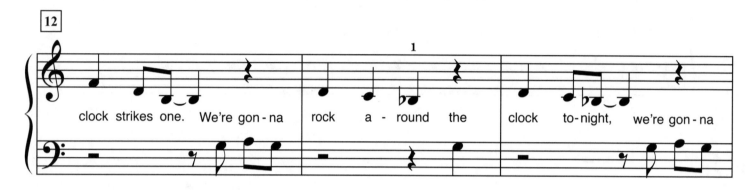

clock strikes one. We're gon-na   rock a - round the   clock to-night, we're gon-na

(duet continued)

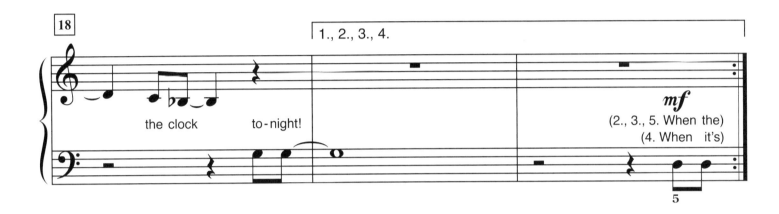

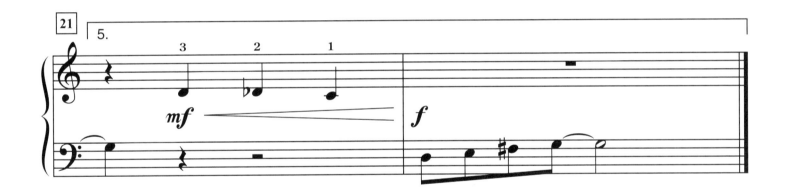

2. When the clock strikes two and three and four, if the band slows down, we'll yell for more.
We're gonna rock around the clock tonight, we're gonna rock, rock, rock 'til broad daylight.
We're gonna rock, gonna rock around the clock tonight!

3. When the chimes ring five and six and seven, we'll be rockin' up in seventh heav'n.
We're gonna rock around the clock tonight, we're gonna rock, rock, rock 'til broad daylight.
We're gonna rock, gonna rock around the clock tonight!

4. When it's eight, nine, ten, eleven, too, I'll be going strong and so will you.
We're gonna rock around the clock tonight, we're gonna rock, rock, rock 'til broad daylight.
We're gonna rock, gonna rock around the clock tonight!

5. When the clock strikes twelve, we'll cool off, then start a-rockin' 'round the clock again.
We're gonna rock around the clock tonight, we're gonna rock, rock, rock 'til broad daylight.
We're gonna rock, gonna rock around the clock tonight!

Star Wars
(Main Title)

Music by **JOHN WILLIAMS**

Arranged by Tom Gerou

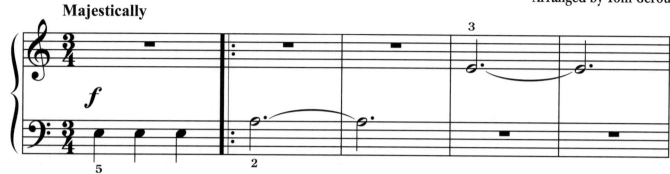

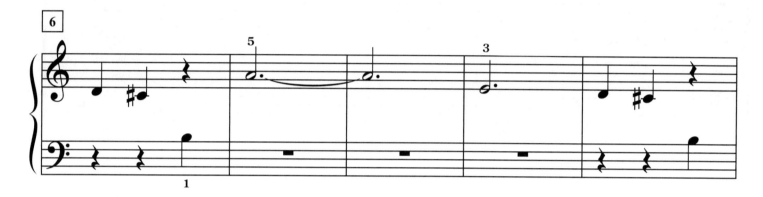

Optional Duet Accompaniment (Play solo part 1 octave higher than written.)

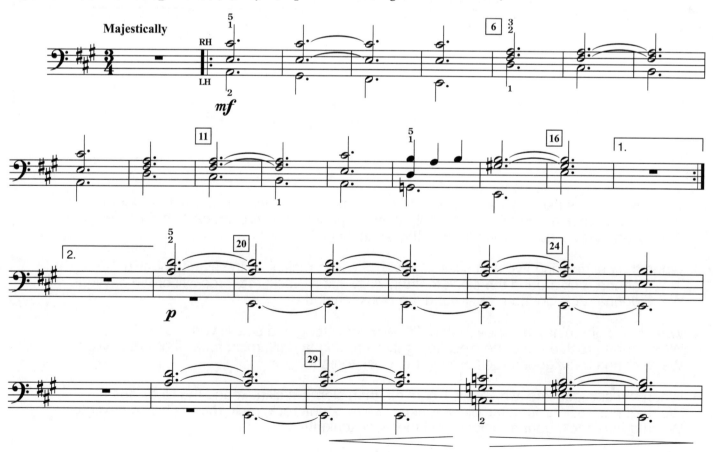

(duet continued)

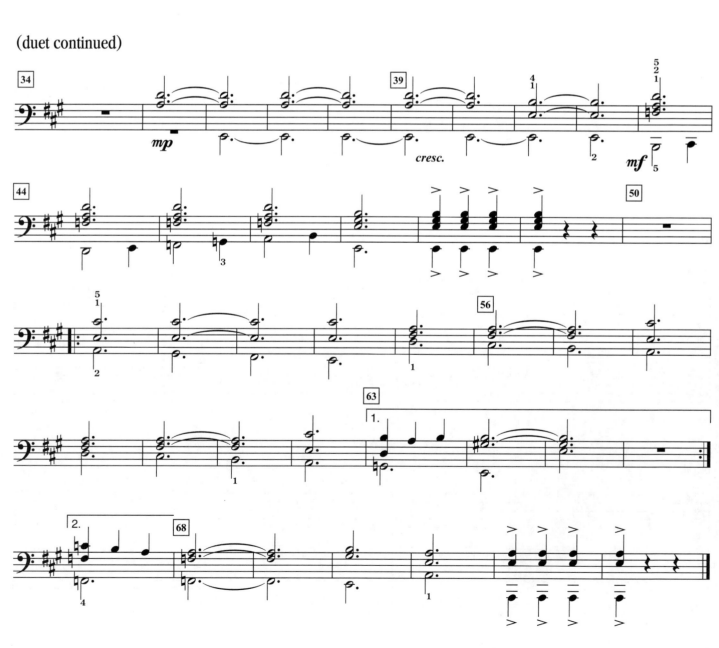

We're Off to See the Wizard

Lyrics by E. Y. Harburg, Music by Harold Arlen
Arranged by Tom Gerou

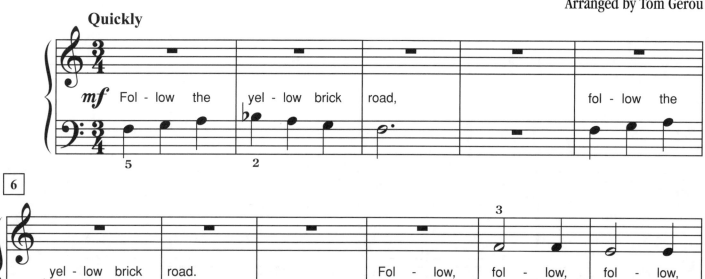

Optional Duet Accompaniment (Play solo part 1 octave higher than written.)

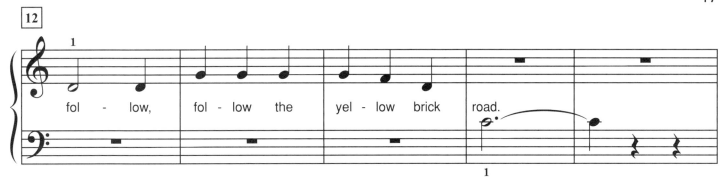

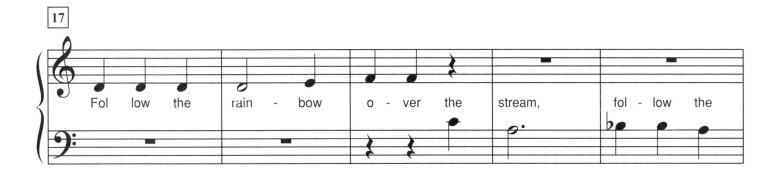

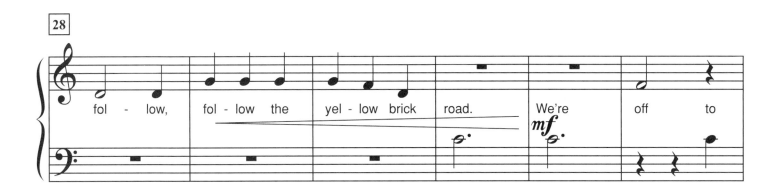

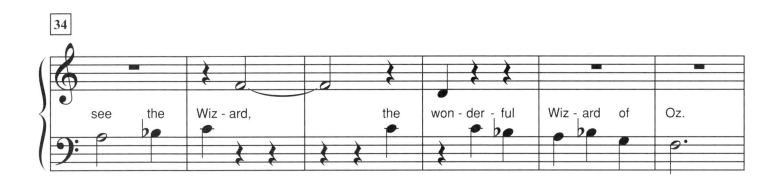

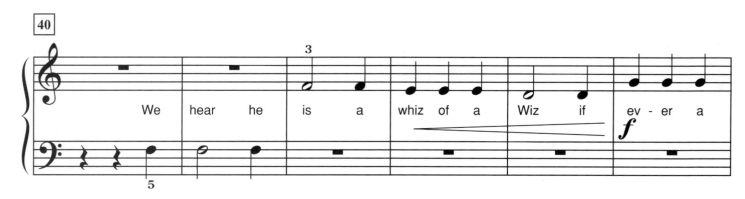

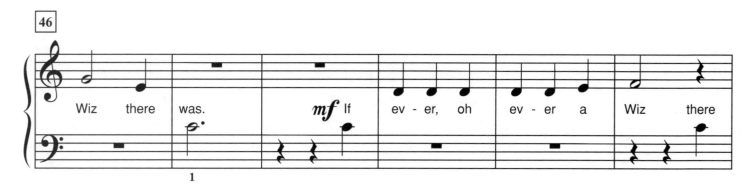

(duet continued)

49

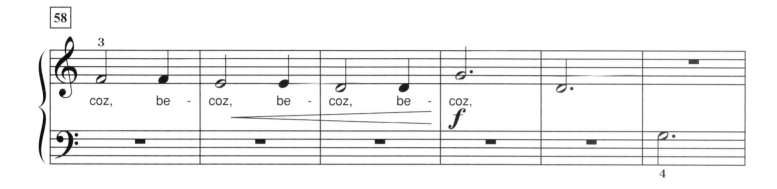

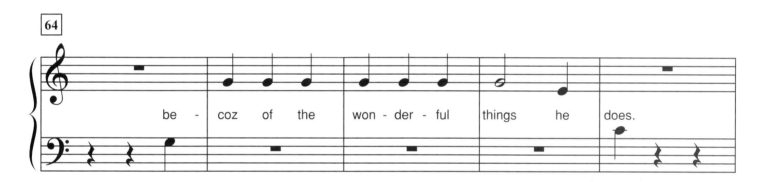

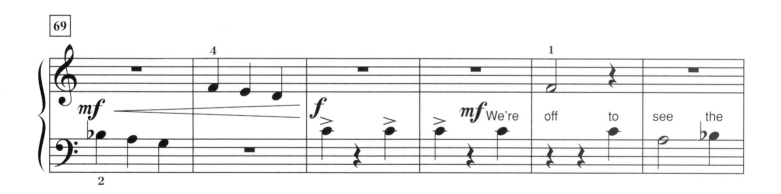

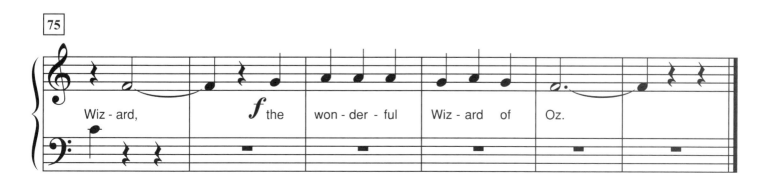

Wipe Out

By The Surfaris

Arranged by Tom Gerou

Optional Duet Accompaniment (Play solo part 1 octave higher than written.)

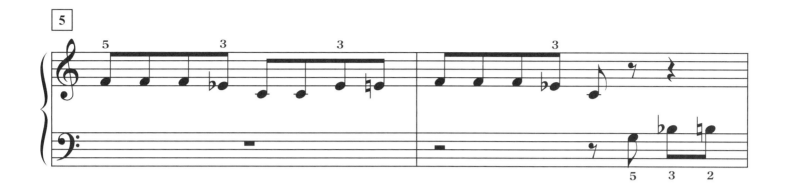

The Wind Beneath My Wings

Words and Music by Larry Henley and Jeff Silbar

Arranged by Tom Gerou

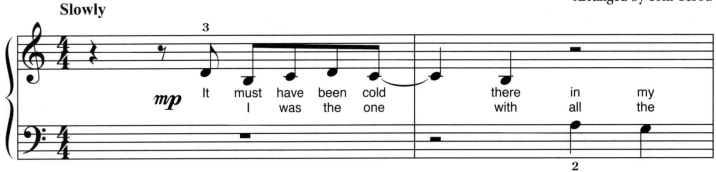

Slowly

It must have been cold there in my
I was the one with all the

Optional Duet Accompaniment (Play solo part 1 octave higher than written.)

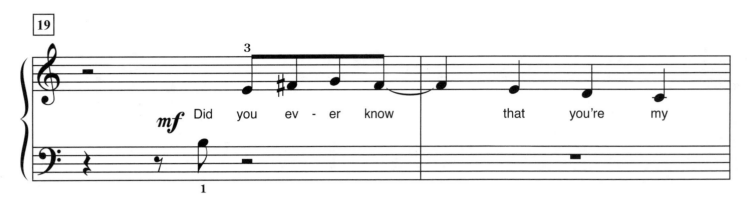

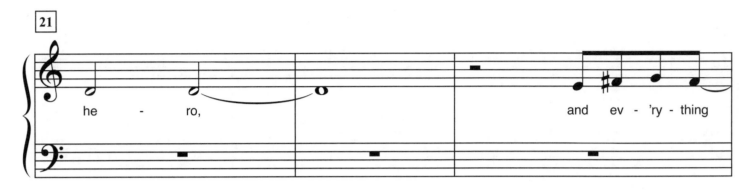

(duet continued)